Ordering Information: Quantity sales. Special
discounts are available on quantity purchases by
corporations, associations, and others. For details,
contact the author at the address above.

Printed in the United States of America

ISBN: 978-0-578-45504-4

Cover art by: Darius L. Knight

Edited & Designed by: Renée Purdie

DEDICATION

If there is anyone who's made an impact on my life and is part of my reason to be at this point in my life it is my mother **Christine Jackson** and her Mother, my Grandmother, **Ida Mae Buffington**. My Mom acted as a spiritual counselor and guide, and my grandmother always told me and taught me to stay encouraged no matter how things may look. She taught me how to appreciate the downs as well as the ups because you can't have one without the other so I should never be discouraged when unsuccessful or too humble to not enjoy success.

R.I.P
Maximus Cooper
&
Jessica Williams

Both Maximus Cooper and Jessica Williams lost their lives to asthma which is a serious problem that I would love to end. His Father who is my older brother, Brandon Jackson, has epilepsy which is also another issue I feel is unresolved, pacified and unaddressed, and I feel this too must come to an end.

PREFACE

This book of poems was stirred up out of emotions and different perceptions of self as a young black man in Amerikkka—not only perceptions related to this country but also to the things learned and my surroundings and the people I surrounded myself with, both positive and negative as blessings, lessons, and learning experiences. Not having many people to talk to led to the production of the pieces recorded. My aim is to be insightful to others or maybe even give a new perception to someone reading this book. My experiences created these personal pieces that I wish to share with you in the hopes you will relate to the poems and apply them to your life.

Thanks, and enjoy the reading.

CONTENTS

Paper, Pen & Perception

1

ASK QUESTIONS

Why do people never learn from their bad decisions?

Why do people see the problem but don't make the transition?

Why do people want to talk more than they want to listen?

Why couldn't I keep this in my head? Why did it have to be written?

Why do something you know you don't like?

Why jump on people?

What happened to one-on-one fights?

Why kill a man you don't know for stars and stripes?

Why not stay in the house on a Friday night?

Why?

Why not?

2

NO LOVE

What's the point of showing love to a person?

If they don't show it back you're the one left hurting

See it's all about smiles and cries

And if you smile then you'll be left with how's and why's

So before I smile I'll weep …

Why?

Because sometimes you have to become a wolf to protect the sheep

So I hold my love deep in the abyss of the sea only for me to see

But don't get it confused—I'm still cool

But I don't have a friend because they will lead you to the end where there is destruction

So there's no love and I'm my own man trying to get to the promised land for reconstruction.

3

MY OWN

You're my sculpture

You're my art

You're my cupcake

You're my pop tart

You're my sunshine

You're my moonlight

You're my night sky

You're my star-bright

You're my up

You're my down

As a matter of fact

You're my all around

You're the angel from the sky

You're the apple of my eye

You're my friend to the end

You're my lover like no other

You are my everything.

I love you.

4

THE DARK SIDE

My favorite color happens to be black

I used to have a positive mind but that was just to keep my mind off the fact that my life is whack

I try to keep it alive because of my pride but it's hard when your emotions have died on the inside but every day I'm alive

I'm blessed but cursed because I'm young with stress and it hurts

And I just thought of something … I'm zero because whatever you multiply me with you gets nothing

And then I think crazy shit in my head like maybe people would be better off if I was dead

Because it's about being happy and it isn't about the money

I was asked why do I smile and I told them because shit isn't funny.

5

READY

Get ready get set let's go! I'm looking forward to the future because the past is reckless

All you see is violence, evil, wrongdoing and corruption and it steady builds like an eruption

And it's all in the population when I look up at the yellow ball I relieve my frustration

If it's my will keep the Smith & Wesson like Will for the demons it's protection

We had an election, history, let me be proud for a second

We got a black president this suppose to be the best country but what's wrong with our medicine?

You don't know because the TV lies, propaganda is my evidence.

Everybody got dirt on their hands so when will you turn on the faucet and let 'em rinse.

6

WHAT I KNOW

I know this,

The blocks of large buildings and broken pavement

Dudes who haven't evolved

So I call 'em cavemen

I know this, I'm not a part of the earth

But the sky

I'm high in my mind

I'm above but I'm not the judge

I have no expression

Because hate is the new love

Every single out here trying to make a dollar

Life is like the Apollo

If your act sucks you're getting pulled by the collar

7

HUMANE

In my head

Imagination unleashed piece by piece

Coming together

To create what's unique

In my hands

Tools that are to be used

For creations in vast variations

Within my heart

Courage, emotion and love

Open with communication, understanding and hugs

I am human

Because I can admit my mistakes and flaws

And still show love for all

Even when they act perfect.

8

MR. LONELY

It seems at times

There are a lot of people around me

Like all these people equal up to a sum

But in the end

I am the only one

But sometimes

I want two or more

But I always find myself

Back at the self-centered core

At least three or four in the circumference

But at the end

I always end up

With feelings of no abundance

Like I need baking soda

Even though I'm the coke substance

What you know about being alone?

From having a lot of contacts

To having no one to contact on the phone

That's why I feel strongly

That I am alone

See, it's hard to establish the real

When you always around the phony

So I'm gone

Just call me Mr. Lonely

9

SCHOOL

When you walk in the building

I hope you have a pair

We all know life

And we know he isn't fair

But the classes don't care

Cuz they ready to judge

With a look or a stare, also

With the contents of your hair

But it really is a grudge with themselves

I'd rather learn; pull up a chair

And with them it's a grudge that impales

They don't feel or see the pain

Now it's wherever you stay

Determines the gang

And to me it's funny

Because of the dudes who claim to have "swag"

They just swag-less with money

So what you rather be?

A money getting fool or a low wealthy dude

Who's about to use his mind as a tool

And with these tools he will build an empire

And them same fools

Will be the ones looking for hire

10

THAT'S CRAZY

You have the chance to get paid

But you rather get laid…

Cool

Don't listen, now you saying "D'oh!"

Like Homer Simpson

And you still don't have a job

And now you're viewed as a slob

Who's penny pinching

Begging and asking

Then when you caught with your hand in the
basket you're viewed as a fool

Because you didn't want to do what you

Were supposed to

Now the people in the hot tub

Don't even want you in the pool

11

SMILE

1, 2, 3 say cheese on the pizza we eat

Seems like there's a different feeling when I see
just a little bit of those 32 teeth

Everybody got 8 fingers

some can't even put up 2 just to say peace

Out and about I'm a plant like everyone else but

I'm trying to sprout

To be happy, smooth, funny cool

I guess I get that from my roots

The vibe to be humane alive I strive before the
day that I die.

Live your life and smile

12

MY FRIEND

My friend is here

My friend is there

My friend is everywhere

My friend is cold

My friend is lethal

My friend is pure

My friend is peaceful

My friend is hate

My friend is nothing

My friend is love

My friend is something

Who's your friend?

13

TRUTH & LIES

They say the truth shall set you free so the lies we believe in is a way to enslave our people ...

To me, lies hurt, they burn and the truth is cold, cool that can heal because of what it stands for which is real.

A lie is like a dream when you are asleep and I don't believe in lies so you can say I have insomnia because I haven't slept in weeks ...
I stay woke.

14

GOD'S WORK

I was told you have to be in tune with your spirit
to actually believe in a miracle

I think it's true because of the almighty imperial

Like butter seeing a miracle is like watching God
work, it's beautiful like a butterfly that flutters,

Just waking up is a miracle for me
I can look up at the sun and it doesn't hurt my
eyes so I feel like there's something better for me.

A miracle is a blessing in disguise to a degree but
it's only a disguise if you don't open your eyes so
you can see.

15

WHO ARE THEY?

Who are you to try and judge?

Who are you to say you are right?

Who are you to hold a grudge?

Who are you to say only I might?

Who are you not to believe?

Who are you to disrespect?

Who are you to challenge my intellect?

You're a nobody.

16

MYSELF ONLY

Now if I'm going to do it I'm going to do it for
myself because worrying about other people isn't
good for the health

I guess you can say that I'm a nice guy so they see
me as a nice try

But I'm tired so don't talk to me unless you saying
that I'm hired

And I'm trying to move forward but I'm stuck in
my ways

But why would I be cool with a snake that wasn't
even cool in the bible days
what I write is historic like a tribal cage under all
that slick talking there's a lot of rage

Because of all the goofiness left and right
but I'm a step up like I'll take the fight

I guess you can say I'm a young Calvin Brock

And when it's all said and done people are going
to be like "Why they call you master?"

And I'll just reply because I know I have it locked.

17

HOW DO YOU DO?

How do you keep cool?

How do you stay low-key?

How do you recognize a fool?

How do you trust the police?

How do you avoid stress?

How do you learn more?

How do you be your best?

If your mind is key,
how do you open doors?

18

THE GUN

The illegal immigrant that no one can stand

But I'm the same immigrant that was created by man

And I'm the perfect fit for anyone's hand

And I came here to protect

But I've been used to see the worst of people's body, face, and neck,

For the dumbest reasons.

19

BLACK PEOPLE

We are the best

We are better than whoever never less

We are strong

We are history in the making

So the history lives long

We are black but don't forget the red and green

We get stereotyped that we can't do any but we can do everything so what does that mean?

We stepping out that box of just dance and sing

But here's something I can believe

We black in America but we have that ancestor in us all to succeed.

20

HOW SHE ACT

I love females because of what they can offer and
their details

I mean I care for you that's why when you ask
questions I tell the truth

Like a young man no more to say except you play

Because when I think I'm about to get on a boat to
a good relationship you sail away

And you I can't reach now I'm stuck on this beach
spelling out S.O.S but still no one has come yet

Quiet no sound you open up to me and you tell me
how's he's a clown

I tell you and show you that I'm your everything
and I'll go down

We use to be face to face, eye to eye but then you
turned around
why and how?

YOU SHOULD KNOW

I might seem cool but don't get it twisted for I can get it in

You can catch me skinny in all black looking like a paper mate pen

If you can't understand the poem then you don't understand real pain most kids love it when it's sunny but I love it when it rains

And I don't like my eyes to be seen when I wear a fitted hat and life is like a maze and I'm the laboratory rat

And I'm trying to go to heaven because it's hell on earth and since I'm on this land how do I trust a church?

And this is what I be thinking more than what I'm feeling
I'm tired of being the good guy so imma play the villain

And please don't ask why
Just take the cards God dealin'.

22

QUESTIONS

By: Brittany Warren-Giles

Questions go around my head with ... Why?

Tears on my pillow as I ... Cry

Makes no sense for us to say ... Goodbye

Impossible to have this pain ... Inside

Thinking about the time we shared makes me
wonder if you even ... Cared

Feels as if I'm stuck in a maze ... With no way out,
I think I'm.
Going. Insane.

So alone without you ...

The question that still remains is ...
Can I still breathe?

23

TRAIN-WRECK

By: Brittany Warren-Giles

You wonder ... I wonder ... I have been wondering
since the year "07"

Didn't understand why you left ...

They told me you didn't want to leave ... I didn't
want you to go,
I wish I could turn back time in order to be your
hero, because you were always mine.

At least you said goodbye ...
Oh wow! You can't because you are asleep ...
Speak ... Speak.

Look at me I am talking to myself ... I am a train-
wreck

You know yesterday I thought of going with you
... As you noticed ... Hopefully you did ...

But I know you didn't ...

I'm talking to myself because you are asleep and
I'm a train-wreck ... With tears in her eyes
because you're gone

And didn't say goodbye!

24

CLEAR THINKING

Where I'm at I see things more clearly

People act funny and that's only because they fear
me

And fear will be the reason that you don't make it

I show love but they still don't take it and that
just shows the power of hatred

But I believe in creation to be able to say that I
made this and instead of Facebook look at the
truth and face this

And I'm not crazy I just say what I think
females are fruit, money is vegetables, life is water
and every day I take a drink

Because if you don't you'll dehydrate and
sometimes it's not what you know but who you
know and there's more friends on myspace

Some people ignorant
so I look at them sideways

I'm just trying to play for keeps and get my earn
I'm talking that paper, money longer than
sideburns and skyscrapers so go ahead and do you
just patiently waiting on my turn.

25

BIGGER THAN ME

I write this poem to show I'm still living to fill out
my legacy

So please in peace let me be
I claim no religion but yet I'm spiritual

I write so much it seems like a ritual so what I
write is now invisible

But still I'm seen watching out for the lies,
Keyword: Project Blue Beam

Watch the devil because he's busy disguising
things to look pretty but I see the ugly truth

So, I write not only for me but also for you

And I haven't been anywhere lately so in my mind
I explore
sky high so I can soar and I got a jungle heart so I
let my emotions roar

Because this is what I do and I feel kind of sad
because of the way I think and I feel it's few like
me but nobody's like me because my mindset is
type A and the rest is type B making a change
doesn't seem likely
Why?

Because people stuck on the same page but they
need to read some more books and see we all
living in a jungle under the same cage

And everybody needs help but how can you get it
if you don't help yourself and it starts with love
too how can you love somebody else if you don't
love you? It's not possible and if you think so
you're confused
blown fuse.

26

WELCOME TO SPACE

I'm trying to get there and that's the place that
everybody fears

It's a place I like to call out of here

A place where no one can be judged it's just space,
lights, and love

Far out and above too
cool, groovy
surrounded by so many stars you would think it
was a movie but no

This is a place of beauty where you can hang loose
like pants without Ryan's belt suspended

By gravity so there's nothing to be felt but
yourself
So far gone it seems as if time starts to melt until
there's nothing left

But to the left and right there are several specks
of light, some dim, some bright

Some small and some big in my eyes
This is cool you dig? Like dirt to a shovel to get
away from it all I hop into my space shuttle

And blast off to art a place where there is no finish
or start

No beginning or end just colors and circles that
spin around me again and again.

27

INSPIRATION

It's all around me so it's the reason why I do it
every day
I inhale it so it's now in my fluids and for me to
avoid it would be foolish

Reckless and out of control so I keep it together
which helps separate the mind from soul

Black is beautiful you need us like a ship needs
coal and I need it like a wheel needs road

So I can go with this poetry that is injected in the
people for the people so what I write is the bevel
piece of a needle

So my plan is to reach the sky so I fly high like
birds or a beetle

And when I feel the bullshit piling
I just close my eyes to see water leading to the
island so that's the reason why I act silly but I
don't play which leads to me writing colors called
poetry

Art of what I say so now the paper has been
painted like a person who's undecided in the mind
I'm steady changing and evolving

And that is why I came up with a resolution

Worry about me and not the pollution because I'm ecofriendly but people not friendly

But I don't care because they just help install it in me.

28

SLEEPY

I'm tired of pretending

I'm tired of the lies

I'm tired of the chances

I'm tired of tries

I'm tired of excuses

I'm tired of the goofy shit

I'm tired of people talking stupid

I'm tired of people being the same

I'm tired of being judged

I'm tired of moving so I sit still and don't budge

I'm tired of being tired and I'm tired of people
being hired just to once again be fired

I'm tired of grown folks acting like children and
believe it or not I'm tired of my emotions and
feelings

I'm tired of the reality of multiple casualties

I'm tired of the same mode
I'm tired of the same old but still I'm awoke so I
stand tall like a tree ...Oak ...

So for Pete's sakes, if you tired like the rest then throw a slumber party and stay woke for the next morning

Because I know I'm up for the money because sleeping is boring.

29

MARTIAN

I don't understand why so selfish?

Around them I feel like a fish on land

I have no help so I help myself with an extended hand and school wasn't my thing trying to be the same was so uninteresting

So if you don't have the right character then you're not on the scene

No caps lock or caption in all caps she would say she's WIFEY type if you ask her but those are actors

Who are just reading off a scripture and I must be a photographer because it seems like I'm the only one who sees the big picture

In which is framed with me as a lame

Because I was a $100.00 dude who made change so I must be a Martian because of how I'm always marked weird or strange

But that's just fear because we're not the same.

30

BEAUTIFUL LOVE

Love is beautiful
Here's my explanation

When you know there is someone you can talk to
when there's frustration

And if you smoke weed you don't have to because
they're your elevation

And when you're alone with them cuddled up
that's your meditation

And fellas you don't mind waiting patiently to
take your train through her tunnel to get to the
train station

And when you leave that person they're happy but
sad like a high school graduation

And you leave them with that feeling like, I got to
have them and when you get them you're happy
like congratulations

And with them there's no irritation

But when you both are close or touching it's a
sensation
no complication

And you both tell each other everything, no
abbreviations

And then you start to think this is the one I want
to have my multiplications together until
evaporation

DIDN'T THINK

I never thought that I would bump into my lover
Such a small world, just call me Woody and you
can be my cowgirl

So we can blast off to beyond and infinity
I can be your one and you can be my trinity

Me and you sound like a possibility

I never thought I would get back into poetry

But because of you I am able to express myself so
openly

Yeah, I'm Urkel and yeah you're Laura
Yup "Oh Laura" I love your ego and your aura

Always truthful no bullshit and if I had a nickel
for every time I think of you I would be rich.

32

WHY SO SERIOUS?

A lot of people walk around mad and I don't know why I can be mad and give up but still I try

Don't get me wrong it's stuff that can make you pissed but if you aiming for the stars frustrated when you finally shoot that anger can make you miss

And that was your only shot now your face red, ears smoking like a tea kettle or boiling pot

And your anger will lead you to rock bottom yourself is what's the problem

Question, Why so serious? Just asking because I'm curious
Being upset has made you imperious leading to becoming delirious

So lay back and relax or that chip on your shoulder will kill and destroy you early so there is no getting older.

33

CHOICES

Life is about choices.

Burger or steak,

Green or blue, fast or slow,

High or low, live or die, go or stay

All of your choices

Bring or take

Away another day.

34

WHAT IS REAL?

Is the truth all around us?

I believe so.

Why?

Because everything around us is a lie

This is just something I be thinking

When somebody says they discovered something
It was really just a secret uncovered my brother

They say the greatest resource is oil but what
about the mother?

How do you contrast fair from fine?

This the matrix man was designed to destroy
mankind but that's only if we let it

What is real?

Is it real because you can see and touch?

Whatever the answer it really doesn't matter
because when you die all the things you see and
touch starts to scatter ... Real or fake?

35

LIES

Don't say you will unless you will because if you say you do but then you don't ...

First off why would you say you will when you know that you won't?

See if you lie then you steal and if you steal then you lie so don't try to play it off like you're the victim when you really think he weak imma get 'em

See this is the mind of a snake and a snake still doesn't have arms or legs to this date, how do you look at yourself in the face?

So I don't trust you because of how you try to change the pace of the race because when you lie there's a change in the heart rate then your pupils dilate

Just from the words that you say and if you do this to the wrong person these lies can give you away now you're gone just from the lies
You're dead wrong.

36

DIFFERENT

I feel like no one understands me,

At first I was like it couldn't
but then I was like it can be

Because I'm my own man

We, are just nothing like the rest I'm talking me
myself and I as an individual

Because if you don't have your own mindset it's
critical and you got it wrong if you thinking
physical

I'm on a different level I'm meaning spiritual I feel
my soul and not my flesh life isn't a game but a
test

So I'm trying to score high as I be getting most of
these people's minds are imprisoned

But because of my third eye I have complete
vision just read what I'm saying you don't have to
listen

I just ask for God to bless me and I feel He
granted me His permission

All real no fake all I'm saying is life about choices
and the decisions that you make.

37

LATE-NIGHT
LIKE STORY

Introverted version of a person too oblivious and
focused to spend my time lurking unless I feel you
worth it slash perfect

Through your imperfections aroused by your
drive and intelligence my soul is erected then
emotions are projected in different directions
Every day awake is another resurrection

I hope that your soulful, eat you like soul food,
mentality is hopeful

When it seems hopeless let's hang sometime from
the tree that is rope-less
Black girl you the dopest

The Jane to my Tarzan, king in the jungle
The bee to my bumble
Let's catch one another when we stumble

Yin to my yang, that's balance to remain humble
Mind is a 4 million puzzle piece of a heart crushed
and crumbled

Let's build royal tunnels that lead to the castle of
what matters
Success is created through practice

With positive patterns to make chapters last
happily ever after.

38

NEW TIMES
SAME CLOCK

Dabbing is the new swagger

And sauce is the new dab

My dab is the new elements of spiritual
enhancement

Can't grasp?

Then just leave it on my tab then

She getting passed around like the collection
plate, too many eggs in one basket

Just tryna get baskets make balling the habit
Life is the tournament where different statuses
and classes determine where you stand in the
brackets ...

Are you lacking or cracking? Or slacking on your
mac'n getting pimped by the master and his
masses.

INSPIRED
THE ALIEN

Successful people inspire a young brother like me
who came from a long wait
Learned to negotiate and instigate but that's the
wrong way like being only into mating without
being inti-mate

Out of wedlock I was born ten toes down, finger-
four got my legs locked
Leader like myself less listened so I'm conformed
to demonstrate

Yet I'm pending cuz my patents aren't just a
giveaway

Astral travel is the perfect way to get away from
the absence that's on the planet rarely making
captions

Verbal I just sip my herbal that's a verb back to
action to find my circle out the crop made by the
u.f.o.
I'm u. f. Urkel ...

Greetings! Setting up meetings for allegiance
that's depleting the humans that are big fat
meanies meanwhile in the meantime

Of making memes in my head I'm dreaming about one of my characters named Dreamy she's dangerous when she's thinking

Can't wait to have suits in the room all in agreement.

40

DISCONNECTED

Sometimes it feels like in real life things aren't real nice or retrievable or believable when the word lie lies in the word believe that seems to be deceiving and misleading to the people too. The higher the expectation the harder the impact so the lower the fall the less damage caused so the fear of change remains intact so imagine the life of a dreamer in a community where it's hell for us all ... Accepting I'm a failure who's gonna constantly fail cuz I'm not perfect right? Worthless it's not worth it right? So I'm less confident while giving more compliments to the less creative more dominant feeling sorry for myself cuz nobody else will nobody else skilled in my training of thought yet what does that matter to an egotistical mad hatter hard to get me or reach me like the hand with no back scratcher passion burning in my soul may be hell bound returning back to burning ashes over the sea my dreams scattered heart and brain both beaten and battered and hammered big kid like my last name Jackson cuz at an early age had to jump out them pampers without any answers like complacency to your master or commander. And I'm still considered A-WOL even though it was everyone else who left like a deadline for a tradeoff and all I get is your hard work is gonna pay off ... When?

When I'm insane or when I'm dead and DMT takes over my entire brain then I unplug completely and can't relate to the wired brain?

41

INSTAGRAM

I wear my heart on my sleeves so there's no filter
so that makes me weirder

But what's weirder being you or walking around
with different filters as if you yourself has
summoned to a shape shifter drifting more into
your image of a picture than what you see in the
mirror

Seeing yourself as pixelated so you filter into
different themes and shades created to make you
look less like the moment of that picture and more
like the pic already saved

In the gallery this a digital tragedy that filtered
surrogate is more acceptable than your natural
blood heritage

Helix is doubled to make u from x and y because
of everlasting love in us yet we don't love
ourselves or another
My sister, my brother

We were made in His image so save that which
doesn't need to be tinted.

42

LET HIM LOVE

Wtf? Wtf? Tell me really wassup

Cuz it's a problem if I say I love you too much

But now you think I don't care if I don't do it enough

Tell me how you feel a connection but we don't stay in touch?

We got a touchscreen for connection but we not connecting

Even Wi-Fi can see we disconnected

But for your love I would dive deep and open clams for that pearl necklace

But I understand if that's unaccepted

43

A FRIEND INDEED

Finding a friend who is a partner is not often

So I'm offering my thoughts up for auction

You need me?

You got me; just pick your options

Exhausted from losses
Rough around the edges
Well them edges I can soften

While bossing

With you under my armpit coughing on armpit

Look what you started

I'm starting to think you the canvas to the artist
New world to the Martian so let me explore that,
adore that

Take you out Lakeshore that

And you know something missing so you can
restore that when you see pain I wanna show you
where the joy at

Cuz it's something about you
Are you 'bout it, 'bout it,

Baby, I don't doubt you

Because I'm so for you that I wouldn't know how
to.

44

PEDRO MEET PIERRE

Never fake it to make it

Just make it

And treat yourself

Don't cheat yourself

No masturbation

But that's how you beat yourself, be yourself

You can be your own worst enemy

Don't need me to help

Everybody got issues

We all need some help

Searching for my higher self

Feels like I've been here before

Shout out to my prior self.

45

SUPREME BEINGS

Dominant consciousness

Got the oppressor viewing black as ominous

I laugh at that comic shit

If the leather glove doesn't fit, you must acquit

Get a grip if you can handle it

The genetic differences

Is the reason you're sentimental out your mind

Cuz we infinite

Bigger dick

Getting intimate

Making love to the universe

Until they silver spooned the earth

But we gone fix it with no whippings or lynching
from trees

And we still suspended, defying gravity

Why you mad at me?

Cuz I come from your majesty

Avidly surpassing beef?

YOU BE ON MY MIND

Damn I can't sleep

Young and restless

Don't wanna press like I'm sweating

So I keep it chill wishing for a text message

No sexting

You just left an impression that I find impressive

Cuz I'm usually defensive

Depressed, passive, less aggressive as protection

So I usually don't do this

But now making an exception

Cuz you may just be the blessing

To relieve my anxiety when I'm stressing

How I'm not the greatest yet or made it yet

Life is a gamble and I'd rather save a check

But you make me wanna place a bet and take a
step

I like you, let's make a date

But I still ain't say it yet

Don't wanna make it awkward

Just wanna do it proper to prosper

So I'm patient, be my doctor.

47

SHARP EDGES

Love shall heal all wounds in due time

Until then

Can you deal with the jagged edges of what's left
of this broken heart?

Your fingers may be sliced from handling sharp
edges

That were never meant to be … need bandages?

Do my sharp edges create too deep of a cut?

Which may make you wanna give up

Or continue to sweep broken pieces

Even though you may not get it all

And get glass in your feet

Pinch and squeeze for relief

So there's no more of me, under your skin

Can you deal with the broken pieces?

Or is this the end

Before the healing begin?

48

QUEEN KIMMIE

Something about you

Makes me ask the question how to?

Cuz all I want is for my intentions to surround
you

Whether I'm with you or not around you

So astounding, grounded too

You can deprive me of my thirst

And make me thirsty

Subliminally hounding you while keeping cool

Queen on a royal stool

While I help, you produce a smile or two

No dentistry

Yo chemistry

Queen Kimmie bee

Got me thinking of crowning you.

WHAT'S AFTER NOW?

Tell me what it is, what else, what is left

Cuz I cannot see next ...

Inject ...

My heart numb so that is the feeling that is left

Can't blame you for not trusting me

Cuz I don't trust myself

When my answers are right I still go ask for help

For finding myself and my true nationality

And that's the noble drew nationality

Can't be rational with the truth of reality

Setbacks and casualties, won't let that define me

So I'm fined by the same bottle of wine that was
spilled

Don't be mad at me

Cuz I'm covered in the blood and placenta

Meet the new member not liked by the members

Who remembers the guy who never was simple

But made things so simple for future investors

Events I don't enter

Cuz of janky promoters in Modesto

I don't trust the vendors

Everyone real

But really projections and holograms in each
other's lives

As we exit and enter

Created in His image

So we all just living images projected into space

That's what we call living

So who's really pretending?

The matrix gimmick was giving

But call me crazy I get it,

But I rather be crazy than brain dead and
mentioned

Abiding by my own decision

To ascend past comprehension

Even though there will be very few to join

And I will be looked at different

Causing tension

But that's balance to the mathematician.

50

INDECISIVE

Somewhere in between

I'm perfect and I'm worthless

Somewhere in between

Serve and I deserve it

A king and a servant, perfected and imperfect

Somewhere in between

Mortal and immortal, dimensions and portals,
radical and cordial

Somewhere in between

A God and a king

Doing it on my own or getting my own team

Somewhere in between

Persistent and inconsistent, never did it and
addicted

Giving up and committed

I feel stuck … I feel stuck …

Somewhere in between

Hatred and love, save 'em all—kill 'em all, even
below and above

Somewhere in between

Help the needy and be greedy, stingy and friendly

It isn't nun and it's plenty

Somewhere in between

I love you and I hate you

Grab my hand let me help you and fuck you bitch,
I can't save you

Cain and Able

I'm struggling and I'm stable

I feel stuck … I feel stuck …

51

FAKE FUNERAL

Just imagine if I died …

How many real eyes realize

Tears overpowered cheers, claimed to be missed

Kiss my rear as I cross over

Allen Iverson: gone from the backwards
environment

Who cherish nothing more than a phat ass

Bouncing up and down doing somersaults as I
catapult

Signing and launching off a world

Where killers are respected, intelligence is
neglected

Deflected and deflated, hated cuz it ain't negative

So you must be doing something positive

It seems like when you rest in peace

That's the way the honest live

Surrounded by the downers

Tried to roll away from my circle getting rounder

As the past follows without following rules or
mottoes

Cuz the pill to set you free seems too big to swallow

Like a mouthful my living has you doubtful

Funny how that person died

But you made the shit about you ...Why I don't trust a soul!

52

JUMPED SHIP

I been left alone all my life

So I now know about neglect and abandonment

So with relations I abandon ships

And back into the shadows of the darkness with the demons

Can't see 'em

Unless my ideas are sparking light bulbs over my head

Blinking like a halo cuz I'm always thinking

Especially when I'm thinking about not thinking

Outside looking in

May look like I'm tweaking

Yet I'm fully conscious of ideas that I'm pondering

To prosper the chosen one.

BE A LADY

Baby girl baby girl

It's hard for me to get you or get with you

When you wanna act like a nigga too

Play your part play your role Billie Jean

Ride with a smooth criminal

Not saying you less important

More important loving and adoring

How you enhancing my performance

In and out the bedsheets

You help me with Adobe and them Microsoft
spreadsheets

So I can see my finances

And my financials are just a couple of examples

Of a partnership, king and queen in chess

Is what it all started with, or started from

So let's return to that

Instead of competing for no reason with each
other

No battle of the sexes

Cuz what gender is the truth that lies naked?

54

LESS IS MORE

Gotta dream it to live it

Cuz being alive just isn't the same as living

So that's the shit that makes me livid

And view life as senseless

If you don't wanna see me do good how can I not
see you as a threat?

We call it competition

You call 'em leaders when they not absolute

Giving no kind of vision

Call them individuals

But they all given the same mission

I just meditate 'til the sun hits the horizon

The earth's lining enlightened

By the spark of Martial and Moorish science

Mighty morphing timing into my own reality

And the way I design it, I have to find my own
alignment

If you done with your work

Hope you can help me with my own assignment

Cuz I can get so lost in my own work it becomes a finding

Some of my finest work

Without crying grapes whining

Thankful for the creative expression of my mind, body and soul

Are my words making you undress?

Or is it the words that's undressing

Giving you the bare minimum and that's enough

Cuz it's the little things

Fragile and brittle things

I see the big picture so I can't belittle things.

55

TIMMY TURNER

If I was really Timmy Turner

I'd be wishing for a sermon

For Jesus Christ to come and show me

All of the ways to be perfect

Living a crazy life that ain't perfect

Black I'm stereotyped cuz they nervous

I ain't ask to be chosen

Bronze face hair golden

If I was really Timmy Turner

I'd be wishing for a burner

To kill every demon plotting

To hurt good people that's working

Babies and innocent, shit is sick

No, I'm not feeling it

Wish I was limitless

To kill every demon walking

And leave they ass burning.

56

JAY

Shout out to Jesse, that's short for Jessica

No white like the days of a tumbler

Focused on not tumbling into unnecessary extra
stuff

Like feelings

Feeling like get my bundles up

'Til that duffled stuffed chips ruffled

Windy city, heart cold as fuck

So if we do before we love please bundle up

Cuz it's cold on this lonely rocky road

Smoking dabbing with no passenger

So if you ain't sliding with me you ain't riding
with me

So I'm asking you what you presenting to my
presence

Is you wit it or pretending to be consistent

Come around to be resistant or persistent

Cuz you get it like deodorant

You sticking or just in my business

To spit it like he ain't shit

Let me tell you while I was with him

Or is you trying to build a business

Big picture that isn't finished until you in it

Like Mona listen

I'm asking cuz my passion can be imagined

As all these eggs and rabbits in one basket

Or all these flavors in Baskins

Cuz I'm all or nothing

Cuz being nothing at all is something

Someone like me can't fuck wit like much shit

Dolo hard to trust shit

So is you worth it should I trust it?

Enough said

Cuz I been through enough shit.

57

JOY

Good afternoon my pride and joy how you doing gorgeous?

No time to toy with what I may value as important

Natural source

The black queen researched my resources

To find out you're royal and Moorish

If I have your love and respect

Then I plan to keep it storaged in a storage

You on fire hot as porridge

Pouring in a bowl used for dope

We should toke you know?

I know you don't know me for sho'

To be a show off

I keep it kosher

You dripping boss

I want mo' sauce

If you said break me off a piece

My piece would already be broke off.

58

NEW KNOWLEDGE

Through these tribulations and trials

I try advising a smile

While in the wild

Crown fit for a king

So I'm not lying when God's truth vibrates sound

That says delay

Isn't denial hard for new truth

To be in the crowd of acceptance

When popular with the emotions

In crowd of rejection

Feeling out-casted by the almighty

Everlasting as I watch time pass me by

To pass time I design a smiling mask

When I cry

Asking me and myself, why?

59

YOU IN ME

I had an epiphany

I am unique, there is no one like me

And it might be highly unlikely

That she may be like me or like me

Wanting a relationship with a replica

The female version of I would be you

And we would be one in unison

Wet climaxing to my masturbation

Stressing over my frustration

Infatuated with my innovations

And vice versa

Two words using the same letter

Two circles to create one

Infinite

Seeing me in you is the perfect resemblance of
intimate

Funny how you thinking what I'm mentioning.

PRESERVED ENERGY

More of a texter, than a talker

Cuz why are we talking with audio when visual isn't often

And I'm awful for being thoughtful

Preposterous for thinking of having a connection

With what's anonymous

A bully of love

Funny how there's no conversation unless I'm starting it

Then when I speak on the obvious I'm starting shit

Forgot it wasn't real love only an act

Look at me on my Martin shit

Calling for Tiesha but left with Pamela

But you don't understand it huh?

Let me preserve …

61

ARTWORK

It's funny how she put me on dope artists but had
no artistry

So I couldn't paint our chemistry

So she blamed artless me

But even W.E.B. could see D.W. couldn't author
me

My illustration is hard as aroused pavement

So I'm molded never folding

No carving me

Marbled perfect scared to and scarred for tryna
marvel me DC

You are for I

Find you comically being for not being fond of me

So the colors of sound are valued moor

Like my people's true heritage, which is
astonishing

Abolishment of deep thought cuz you shallow

And can't muster my condiments

Or ketchup to my consciousness

So being called crazy is a compliment in today's timelessness

Ticking away

Options only choosing the option-less

For a spotter creates shooter awkward

Like land to an aqua jet scuba diver trooper super sizer

For a wingless flyer without wings and fryers

But keep it cool like a suit and tire

Rolling in a pool of fire

Swimming in the flames of smoke of Jane

Marry me, here's a ring of dope

And a sugar cane of coke, able to create a clone version

Call it the retarded "G" or retarded Spartan

Fighting for a monarchy

As myself starts mocking me for not knocking me for propping me

To be at the top while she's topless topping me

Until my top start popping like pop when u shake the top

And bottom and let the top release on her face

As she cleans on her soccer knee

Artwork is what I gotta be

To make glaucoma gotta see.

62

COM-ED IN THE BED

Erect entering you

Is plug to a socket

Creating intimacy described as electricity

What a surge when we merge

Hair isn't the only thing standing

Being in your trunk is something I could never forget

Like an elephant

So don't be shocked if I remember every detail of your skeleton

Taste of your liquids

And every spec of your melanin

Hate when your melons in and love it when your apple out

So I can bob for apples

Twist the cap and drink from your Snapple

Pouch when we connect and reset

Like the power grid I'm blacking out.

63

LAST PLACE

Last shall be first and first shall be last

So the beginning of this poem is the ending

Looking both ways before I cross

To make a cross is crucifixion

So did I kill him? Cuz he died for my sins

And I'm still sinning

Got my head spinning

Like I'm in need of an exorcism

Like Rose, wish I could have fucked Emily

Depersonalized mind feeling less of human

And more of an entity

I might not break

But it's rape from the way life bending me
tremendously

As I lie defenselessly

3rd eye stretched wide open

But tell me what's entering?

The ending of the beginning way past limbo

Died trying to live

So afterlife where are you sending me?

Back or forth? Life is transferrable energy.

64

LIFE ITSELF

Been fucked over so much in life

That it's hard for me to trust this life

Like what the fuck is life?

Surrounded by so much hatred

That it's hard for me to love this life

Like; how can I live this life

Without knowing what living like

When everyone living lies

I only know what existing like

But I'm trying to keep faith in life

And not debate this life

And remember it's a pace in life

Without racing life

I just don't want a baby to be the only way of
creating life

Trying to create my life to maybe save a life

Instead of not being shit in life

But shit, it's life …

Cuz most don't even get a life.

65

THAT BODY

You're not a nobody just because nobody knows
you …

You're not a nobody just because somebody "no's"
you …

You're not a nobody because of other opinions …

You're not a nobody because of your position …

If you feel like you're nobody

Just know that nobody can be you …

For you are somebody

And that is a fact that will always be true …

You are somebody no matter what you choose to
be

Because I could never be you like you can never
be me …

But you can be somebody different,

Somebody that makes a cure or makes an
invention …

Are you somebody who does nothing?

Or a nobody who does something?

Tell me …

Are you that somebody?

Cuz the world really needs somebody.

.

66

LITTLE BOUT ME

Learning to listen more and speak less

Has made me soft spoken

Appearing closed difficulty leveled hard

When spoken word is opened

Like the book of pages

Potent like the chemical stages of the gas chamber

Baring my soul like dying in the open for us all to
see

Zero is the only number that gravitates my
understanding

So my fall is free floating in rotation of my
thoughts

My mind is a planet

Insane right until I mention

Grabbed attention

From explaining how that same planet can also
sustain life

So to me

The Big Bang could never explain life.

2K ABLE

My brother, my brother, supposed to be my
brother

Adam was my father, Eve was our mother

Yet still kept the covenant and made sure you
were covered

Even supportive of your fuckery

When you were on some other shit

Like no comment when speaking

The loudest one in the room is your weakness
sneaking

Using excuses for reasons, your transition shifted

Finding mischief in my meekness

But it ends now

Cuz I learned you will later bring death if I don't
defend now

So the relationship must end now

Foot down

As I stand up, better stand down

Because I will kill a boy before I allow a man
down

Broken bond and band now

Cuz my patience you were testing and stretching

Comfortable with me stepping and fetching

Like a dog; spelled backwards is God

And I'm mighty and vengeful

You'll be damned for biting the hand

The same hand that would extend you

Without my blessing, you wouldn't have a
blessing

For your hand to extend to

You ain't shit but an anchor

Holding back my shape

So I'm finna delete you like I'm using the pen tool

But watch how God ascend me

And how He descends you

Nobody to blame but yourself for the shit that you
been through

So don't say you have a brother you're kin to.

C.O.O.L IS LAME
L.A.M.E IS COOL

Careless Options of plotting death on an Opposition living Lawless was her "C.O.O.L"

How she chose to love the heartless

While my thinking is a

Limitless Artistic Mission of the Exquisite

Was considered "L.A.M.E"

So we drifted from differences

Love hanging with killers but GTA was the only mission

She been on to be killing shit

And maybe with fashion and appearances

But I'm the lame head game head

And that shit pushes my buttons

As I level up without cheating

But with these glitches and diversity of backwardness

Makes the difficulty hard when trying to keep a sane head

So I pray to my programmer

To have the stars and mushrooms throwing fire

As I grow big and go hammer

Funny how what she considers cool

Can get you killed

Cuz those words make the "ca" sound

And what you see as lame got me living lavish

Now I "ha" laughing "la" now you confused "ca" saying huh?

Making the what sound

If it's cool not to give a fuck

Don't expect the lame to give a fuck now

Like I'm trying to fit in with the tradition

Funny how the outcast become trending

The ridiculousness of labeling is tremendous.

AS EYE WATCH

Patience is a virtue, impatiently learning to become more virtuous

From the days of the streetlights representing my curfew

Stayed on the porch mapping out a plan for a Porsche

That isn't stolen

In the streets creating a mobile pursuit

Or an arrest for a stolen purse

Used disbursed

Truth of being self-evident for happiness in which I pursue

Declaring independence to not join the streets

That's filled with retaliation and re-vengeance

Watching death play on the corners from a distance

Because my fence represents my boundaries in real life existence

See I didn't jump off the steps yet

Thinking five moves ahead like a chess match

To avoid the setback

Cuz the wrong move on the concrete

Can move bullets forward as your body remains
still

While your brains step back

And that will be the same concrete years later

Where your brains were left at

If these streets could talk they would yell, holler,
scream and weep

War and peace—howling wolves' sharp teeth

Biting through the flesh of whelping sheep

Screaming help for me

While snorting coming from the snouts of pigs

Shooting melanated baby goats

Black kids with a mouth of ribs

While the mistreated, beaten and defeated babies

Are crying in the fetal position

The needle inches in, skin pinching got the addict
screaming

Back and forth with her demons

Sucking, smacking and clapping in the dark alley

Broken glasses moans and groans as the dealer
releases his semen

These are the perks of the streets

Predicted and depicted from the scriptures and
scripts of the pyramids

As the party goer wheezes and sniffs white
crystals

That happen to look or resemble the hieroglyphs

Young girl screaming help! In her mind

As she has unwanted sex

Her body stiff from a drip in her drink

Unseen as she sips

While loud whispers come from a snitch

On the same island looking at oncoming
European pirate ships

2016 angry chants of Black Power

Loud explosions blazing fires

Followed by the shining rising fists

Waves of roars coming from the lion's den

Scribbled writings from the writing pen

Of names captured for FEMA camps

As they sign them in auto tune

Captures the devil's laughter and smiling grin
over the world

Watching from the window as the airplanes drop
bombs

And chemicals over the skies

As it looks like a web from a widow

Truth begins as the lies should end

Now I lay me down to sleep

I pray to the Lord my soul to keep

As I lay on this pillow

BABY BOY

No longer can I be your shadow

Pacify the baby

Or rock the crib when you've lost your rattle

Gu-ga babble talk has me baffled

When you old enough to sit your ass on the porcelain saddle

To handle your business

Not on your shit cuz you sit in it

It is a sickness

You are your own reason for your diaper rash

As your diaper sag

Scared to carry your own weight, little nigga

You can't even be responsible for an empty diaper bag

Your hype is sad

Shooting with no follow through

Baby boy

Life won't baby bottle you

Now wipe your ass.

71

BIO LOVE

I've been doing cross examinations

And these niggas tainted, that's contamination

Fake love

I don't want it and the shit contagious

Catch the cooties?

Call of duty shooting zombies

I can't do it biohazard body suited

President of the quarantine unit

Quarantine Cupid

For he too is infected

The love is ineffective, better yet defective

And I cannot respect it

That's for anybody

I'm the anti-virus, I'm the anti-body

My soul pure, I'm in tune to it and immune to it

Untouched by what the fumes doing.

72

THE CONVERSATION

(Street Nigga to Hood Nigga)

Hard to show respect to anyone, myself or my son you didn't deal with neglect your father didn't run as I chase the streets to find family that understands me even if we fight we gone make up, shake up, and get our cake up by any means necessary selling drugs, killing and stealing because I gotta feed mines so it's him or me keeping the gun as my heat in the middle of my heart which is cold as February you pussy forever scary. See I'll do whatever for family including penitentiary cuz the money more important as I hustle as much as I can before them cuffs clinch and I'm gone and the family missing me see I'm "100" loyal to my set, loyal to retaliation, loyal to the death that came to my gang and innocent but the streets don't stop so I'm in this shit. I'm in the field nigga like a true field nigga with no cotton just a lot of paranoia and gun smoke and marijuana smoke makes the air feel thicker like a thot I can fuck off of a pill I got; then send her on a mission to get my enemies attention as I drill my opp; short for opposition; in a position to get my name up, like my money coming quicker than being broke in a class sitting fuck thinking about a decision no conscience no wonder or pondering thinking too much I made up my mind I'm creating bucks while you scared to get in it but you imitating us faking it to make it like you was whipping up the soda with the baking you was perfect attendance after school with the counselor like a patient you was patient; I ain't waiting I believe what I throw up gang banging for my dead homies you scared to get you some bread homie; that's that lame shit don't claim shit you niggas weirdos cuz y'all not in the streets on that same shit so don't ask who you can hang with; got a pistol but you never popped it please stop it streets love us cuz the streets work you better off dancing in a choir making your feet work talking to the pastor where they preach church. So if you scared go to church nigga and wait on God and see if prayer work nigga while we break down, bag up and make you prey over this work nigga. Ready to risk it all but if you ain't bout it don't get involved.

73

THE CONVERSATION PART II

(Hood Nigga to Street Nigga)

First off I'm not pretending I can relate cuz some days I have bad intentions wishing I could take the easy route killing for profit because of empty pockets fucking with my logic but I got this avoiding nonsense that shit abolished it's hard for everybody to get some knowledge or be self-educated while going to college but it's easy for anybody to catch a body it's nothing but you say I'm fronting cuz off the porch I wasn't jumping but I got something to live for while you niggas living for nothing get the fuck from my circumference gang banging with no structure but claim your toughness but killing innocent people is something I cannot fuck with for I don't find that gangster; you know what's gangster? Choosing not to hang in a crowd for protection as security I can stand on my own two feet where I can influence myself intrigued by my individualism and not a group of impurities with false versions of maturity I refuse to have the blind luring me and allow the devil's plan to keep flourishing so God, growth and development is the only thing alluring me. Blind leading the blind into a pitfall I took the road less traveled while you stuck in the penitentiary pit stop so you pissed off? That same dude you were loyal to with your secrets started whistling and snitching off so his own time in prison can be reduced and clipped off but it's all a part of the system that you are in a cage living not to mention you stuck in a cage while your best friend becomes a father to your daughter and a husband to your woman with no visits while you live with the sickness thinking how you sent letters with no response you were sent off. But somehow I'm soft, I'm gay and it's me you hating because I wear my actual size of pants while you tough sagging yours while your cheeks are out as a homosexual invitation for back door penetration who really faking? See my mind is gangster knowledge stronger than any guns or knives there's good and bad, truths and lies then you had Al Capone and John Dillinger real gangsters that wore suits and ties. See to be gangster is to be a gentleman you simpleton but it's too complex to the less intricate if you confused then you lose with less choices to choose and this is why knowledge rules. See I can take a word and give you the synonym following and you can think was an antonym when it was just the alternate now you think it's many differences so I'm pulling the strings to your life and how you living it cuz there's a non-comparison with fourteen trout to a bigger fish prisons are big businesses and I'm the master so you right stay gangster in that field nigga so you can become my field nigga and work my land to make me money so I can give it back to the families that lost loved ones who you killed nigga.

DEPRESSURE

De-pressure; depression from the pressure is
unmeasured

For it wallows deep away

From the shallow smiling face

That remains unhappy

And dis-pleasured by whatever's bothering

Causing selfish loathing

And the feeling of incompetence

Now Gothic forming into the skeleton locked in
your own closet

Beating on the door for your releasing

Of being something more

But overcoming feels impossible

So confidence is less of an option

When fighting yourself is dividing yourself

The great wall of depression

As you're climbing for help

As I'm trying to help, driving and flying for help

As I wipe invisible tears dried from dehydrated
eyes

Crying for help

I try my hardest with the remainders of breaths

Thinking my caress and touch can lead you back
to your flesh

Feeling and finding yourself

But instead I'm left with less

Trying to give my positivity to the numb

Allows you to hear without feeling me

I'm now hugging death

Your opinion is now viewing "Life is Less"

While thinking less of life, hugging a body with
no soul I felt what death was like in
reality without over imagination from the
experience of a vessel in my arms reminded
me of desecration ...
A living body where the soul was vacant,
nowhere to be located

Her happiness has evaporated

Living with only fabrications of positive situations

So I can't help unless I'm praying that she makes
it

Because I can't allow these energies to become
absorbed and saturated.

75

THE WALKING SOUL

Deep within I was hiding compromising with ego's selfish ways of what was considered reality until faced with the uncertainty of life and close encounters of casualty humbled him to find me the divine me intervention was a gift given so it's time to show you a different living, the harmony of one. Star, moon and sun which is me, myself and I … you, yourself and yours … we, ourselves and ours as I emerge I gain more power to no longer want to be like things but attract like things through thoughts becoming more thoughtful of my thoughts repelling awful accepting all energy from the ant to the sunflower all is one for one can't live without the other third eye widening as I become more self-discovered now looking back I can see how most are sleep spiritually their flesh is the third dimensional cover to keep the soul sedated now awake the longer I stay awakened I can see the hair follicles from point shavings it's amazing and more understandable of God and what it means to not only trust but feel, be and see the intangible and feel vibrations and energies entering and exiting is mentoring me spiritually allowing myself to let my spirit resurface without interfering fearfully but trusting myself skillfully sending questions to the cosmos to get answers from art I ask how real am I looking through transparent skin so the answers become clear to me while having reflections not from a mirror but astral projections finding new connections from being able to be disconnected as I learn these new teachings I respect it and further my journey and my checklist of things I would love to meet and connect with; the feeling was scary at first until I realized my real eye was protected surrounded by love without fear of being rejected makes me want to explore more flying without wings as I soar more. Ernest Rutherford was onto something great when he split the atom I split myself in two creating my own replica "I" used to want money and cash but me and myself understand this is the best wealth for us the more I evolve the more I'm stepping up and coming to the surface of this flesh walking amongst the mortals if only they knew of the portals and powers that reside within then they could be at peace and confide with what wants to be alive again like myself because this isn't Pierre but the third eye within him writing for him better yet with him from another dimension who likes to explore and travel as well. His ego's removed so he isn't glued but instead jumping out of his shell to leaps and bounds project, propel and prevail and this composition is his proposition for you to join him in blissfulness as he remains so compelled in a place where time doesn't exist and your soul can just sail in control of both of the realms what a story to tell … I am … The Walking Soul.

Printed in Great Britain
by Amazon

45023163R00066